A Second Easy Album For Organ

Pavane	Paul Drayton
Scherzo	Alan Ridout
Prelude	William H. Harris
Interlude	David Lord
Saraband and Interlude	Herbert Sumsion
Toccata in Seven	John Rutter

An Easy Album for Organ (6 Pieces) is also available.

Oxford University Press
Music Department, 37 Dover Street, London W1X 4AH

1-95

PAVANE

PAUL DRAYTON

Printed in Great Britain

OXFORD UNIVERSITY PRESS, MUSIC DEPARTMENT, 37 DOVER STREET, LONDON W1X 4AH

SCHERZO

ALAN RIDOUT

8

PRELUDE

WILLIAM H. HARRIS

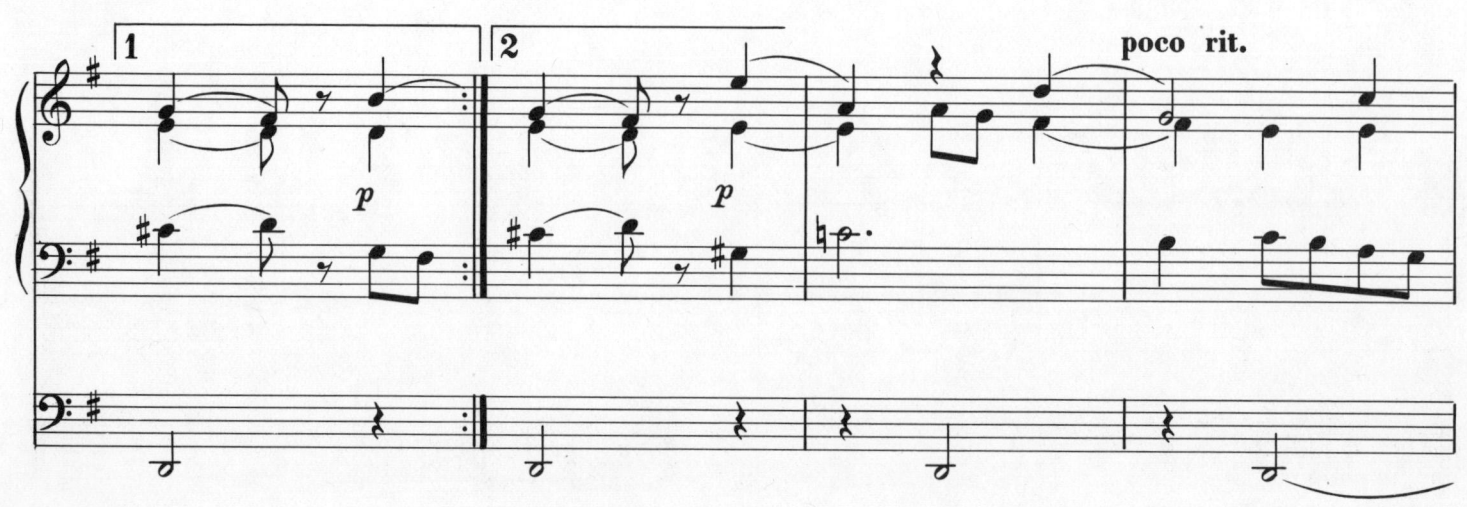

INTERLUDE

DAVID LORD

SARABAND AND INTERLUDE

Poco lento (♩ = c. 72)

HERBERT SUMSION

*or solo reed

TOCCATA IN SEVEN

JOHN RUTTER

TOCCATA IN SEVEN

JOHN RUTTER

Reproduced and printed by
Halstan & Co. Ltd., Amersham, Bucks., England